Archaeology

Copyright © 1988, Raintree Publishers Inc.

Translated by Alison Taurel

Library of Congress Number: 87-28634

  2 3 4 5 6 7 8 9 0   91 90 89 88

Printed and bound in the United States of America.

Library of Congress Cataloging in Publication Data

Archaeology.

  (Science and its secrets)
  Includes index.
  1. Archaeology—Juvenile literature. 2. Egypt—
Antiquities—Juvenile literature.   1. Series.
CC171.A73   1988   930.1   87-28634
ISBN 0-8172-3077-7 (lib. bdg.)
ISBN 0-8172-3094-7 (softcover)

ARCHAEOLOGY

Raintree Publishers — Milwaukee

Contents

GREAT SITES AND
LOST CIVILIZATIONS

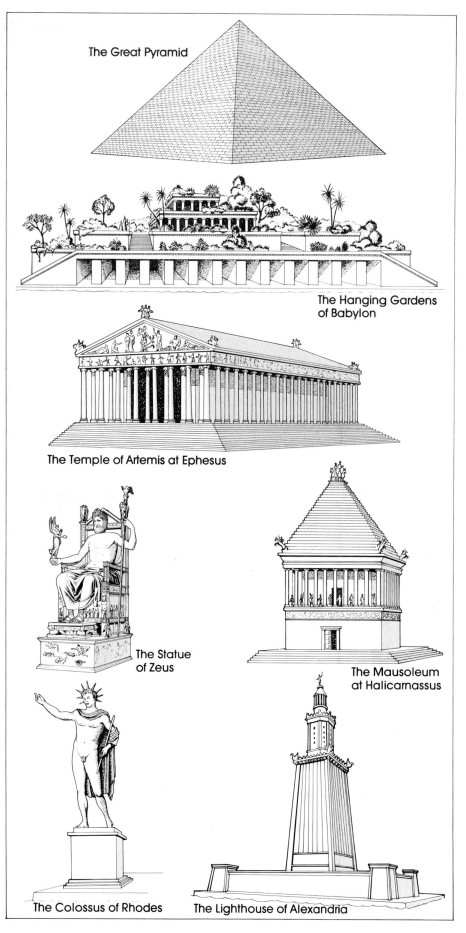

The Great Pyramid

The Hanging Gardens of Babylon

The Temple of Artemis at Ephesus

The Statue of Zeus

The Mausoleum at Halicarnassus

The Colossus of Rhodes

The Lighthouse of Alexandria

What are the Seven Wonders of The Ancient World?

The ancient Greeks and Romans loved to keep remembrances of the marvelous and the extraordinary. They paid as much attention to natural phenomena as they did to exceptional people or buildings. They established a list of statues and monuments which they found particularly remarkable on a technical scale. The lists varied, but seven magnificent wonders are generally recognized as being the most outstanding.

The *Great Pyramid at Giza* is the tomb of Cheops, a king of ancient Egypt. It stands on the west bank of the Nile River outside Cairo. It contains more than two million stone blocks that average two and one-half tons each. Its base covers about thirteen acres. It was constructed approximately 4,700 years ago.

The second wonder is the *Hanging Gardens of Babylon.* They are attributed to a queen and a legend—Semiramis. They were constructed by King Nebuchadnezzar II at the beginning of the sixth century B.C.

The great Greek sculptor, Phidias, who lived in the fifth century B.C., created the third wonder—a gigantic statue of the God of Gods, the *Statue of Zeus.* Made of gold and ivory, it was placed in a temple in Greece at Olympia.

The *Mausoleum at Halicarnassus* is located in what is now southwestern Turkey. It is a tomb for Mausolus, an official of the Persian Empire. When he died in 335 B.C., his wife, Artemis, ordered a magnificent tomb for him. It was 135 feet (41 meters) high. Some of the greatest Greek artists, architects, and

This reconstruction of the temple of Diana at Ephesus dates to the seventeenth century.

sculptors took part in the construction of this fourth wonder of the ancient world.

The fifth wonder is the *Temple of Artemis at Ephesus* in western Turkey. It was built in 550 B.C. and was one of the largest and most complex temples built during ancient times.

The *Colossus of Rhodes,* the sixth wonder, was an immense bronze statue 120 feet (37 m) high. The statue honored the sun god Helios. It was built at the beginning of the third century B.C. and erected at the entrance to the port of the island of Rhodes.

The last of these wonders of the world was the *Lighthouse of Alexandria,* a monument built at the beginning of the third century B.C. It rose above the Port of Alexandria in Egypt on the island of Pharos.

The tomb of Mausolus appears on this engraving.

9

What remains of these seven wonders?

The Great Pyramid is the only one to have survived through time. It is still quite magnificent, but it has lost the limestone coating which covered its sides and made it smooth. It now looks as though it is made up of giant stairs.

We know of the other monuments quite well by the descriptions given by ancient authors. Several representations of the Statue of Zeus, the Colossus of Rhodes, and the Temple of Artemis are on ancient coins. The Mausoleum of Halicarnassus was destroyed in the Middle Ages by the Knights of St. John.

Numerous engravings depict the Alexandria lighthouse, which was destroyed by an earthquake. Excavations undertaken in Babylon have revealed part of the terraces on which the hanging gardens were suspended.

A view inside the Great Pyramid, the tomb of Cheops.

Pyramids loom over the plateau of Giza near Cairo.

Are there pyramids anywhere other than in Egypt?

Yes, the Indians of Central America built structures similar to Egyptian pyramids. But, in general, they were used as temples. Some of them also served as tombs, like the famous pyramid of Palenque in Mexico.

How many pyramids are there in Egypt?

There are several, but Cheops is the largest. Between about 2700 and 1700 B.C., all the pharaohs had themselves buried under pyramids. In some of them the inside chamber walls are covered with inscriptions in Egyptian writing called hieroglyphics. These "pyramid texts" were destined to ensure the immortality of the king and to help him in his voyage toward "the other world."

From the sixteenth century B.C., during the "New Empire," pharaohs were buried in underground tombs. The tombs were dug out of the cliffs. The area in Egypt where the tombs are grouped is known as the Valley of the Kings.

What was the Great Pyramid used for?

Some believe that Cheops' pyramid was used as a religious temple for secret rites. Others think that it was a monument which contained all the great measures of the universe—the distance of the earth from the moon, the radius of the earth, etc. In actuality, it was simply a tomb.

At the base of the Great Pyramid are large gray stones.

What is the most famous treasure ever discovered by archaeologists?

Without doubt, that would be the treasure of Tutankhamen. The tomb of that pharaoh is certainly the richest ever found. The art objects, gold, and jewels number in the thousands.

It is the only pharaoh's tomb dating to fourteen centuries B.C. in Egypt which was found intact. All the others, found in pyramids or in the Valley of the Kings, had been pillaged.

Its discovery by the archaeologist Howard Carter and Lord Carnavon was accompanied by so many disputes with the Egyptian authorities, that its fame was increased even more. And when Lord Carnavon died under somewhat mysterious circumstances shortly after discovering the tomb, people began to talk about the "curse of the pharaohs."

How were the great stone monuments built?

How were the heavy stones transported?

Ingenuity and human patience transported the stones. How did they break apart enormous blocks of rock? They hollowed out holes in the rock and sunk in wooden wedges. They wet the wood so it would expand and make the stone break apart. The stones were then tied with cords and dragged either directly along the ground or on a road of wooden poles. In Egypt, stones could be transported very far on wide boats which followed the course of the Nile.

Scaffolding was used to build the temples and palaces of Mesopotamia, which were all made of brick.

To build the pyramids, long ramps of earth were constructed over which workers could drag the stones. These ramps, which were elevated as the construction continued, were destroyed later.

On the inside of the temples, piles of dirt were accumulated so that the artists who sculpted or painted the hieroglyphics could reach the height of the ceilings and columns. The earth was removed as the work advanced.

The Romans developed technical methods, particularly with the use of some types of cranes.

Two wonders among the many that were found with Tutankhamen's treasure in 1922—the back of the royal chair, showing the young pharaoh and his wife, and the coffin of Tutankhamen.

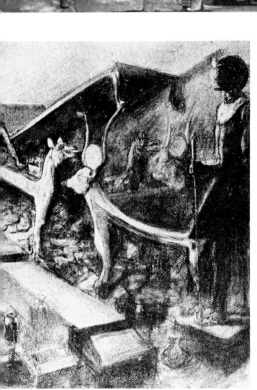

The curse of the pharaohs!

It was the famous English writer, Conan Doyle, the inventor of the character Sherlock Holmes, who first suggested that Lord Carnavon had been a victim of the "curse of the pharaohs." Others who were associated with the project also died, but naturally. And in reality, Lord Carnavon had been ill for some time. Howard Carter, Lord Carnavon's collaborator, who was the first to enter the burial chamber, did not die until years later and under very normal circumstances.

Imagine the wonder of Howard Carter and his companions when they entered the treasure chamber of Tutankhamen's tomb.

13

In 1977, archaeologists discovered a tomb in Vergina in Macedonia. It was the tomb of Philippe II, the father of Alexander the Great.

Have any tombs been found intact?

In Thebes, in the Valley of the Kings, the funeral chamber of Ramses IV (twelfth century B.C.) had been pillaged.

Several archaeologists have had the fortune to find burial chambers, often rich ones, completely or nearly preserved. In Egypt during the 1930s, the Frenchman Pierre Montet discovered royal tombs in Tanis dating from the eleventh to the eighth centuries B.C. Many objects were removed including the pharaohs' silver coffins.

Also around 1930, in Ur, in Mesopotamia, the Englishman Leonard Wooley discovered royal tombs filled with jewels, crowns, costumes, ornaments from harps, swords, helmets, and more, all of gold.

In 1977, Greek archaeologists excavated in Vergina, Macedonia, under an ancient grave and found a magnificent tomb with a facade like a Greek temple. In the underground rooms, they found precious objects —boxes of carved gold, silver vases

Buried statues of the warriors of Chinese emperor Qin Shi Huangdi were recently discovered. Thousands of terra-cotta soldiers are still buried.

decorated with reliefs, crowns, and much more.

It now seems certain that this tomb was that of King Philippe II of Macedonia, the father of Alexander the Great, and his last wife.

The tombs of the people of Scythia, in Pazyryk, at the east of Siberia, have also been explored. They contain materials which are twenty-five centuries old.

In China, one of the most important tombs is that of the emperor Qin Shi Huangdi, who reigned at the end of the third century B.C. The tomb itself has not yet been excavated. But, nearby and underground, the clay army of the dead king was discovered—more than five hundred statues of soldiers accompanied by twenty-four life-size horses.

Who pillaged the tombs?

The majority of tombs have been robbed, often by the same workers who had constructed them. Not content with emptying the tombs of precious objects, the thieves even set fire to mummies which they had removed from the coffins! Robberies continued from age to age. In the last century, and even more recently in Egypt, grave robbers have sold objects of value from the tombs to tourists. To this day, ancient tombs in Italy or burial chambers found in Turkey, Central America, or South America are often subjected to pillage by certain inhabitants of those countries.

For archaeologists, treasures are not limited to precious stones or metals. The paintings of this temple of Bonampak, a lost city in the Mayan jungle, are also an extraordinary discovery.

Emblems found in the Indus Valley.

Can treasures still be found?

What exactly are *treasures* in archaeology? They are precious objects, not only because they are made of gold or silver, but also because the works in clay are testimony to exceptional beauty and art. Such is the case, for example, of vases decorated with black or red figures fashioned by Greek potters.

During the course of excavations, numerous treasures have been found and continue to be found in tombs, hiding places, or dwellings. The town of Pompeii, for example, which was buried in the lava of Vesuvius in A.D. 79 lost a number of riches—objects of gold and silver, bronze and stone statues, paintings, and more.

In all of Europe and Asia, antique coins are still being uncovered. They were buried because of the economy of people who wanted to hide them in case of war or invasion. Several years ago in Afghanistan and Bulgaria, treasures of jewels were found. Most recently in Turkey, an important collection of antique coins was found.

Among the treasures are tablets of clay covered with Assyrian and Babylonian inscriptions. These were the books of ancient times that allow us to better understand those civilizations.

Have archaeologists discovered unknown civilizations?

The biggest merit of archaeology has been to reveal people and civilizations that were either totally unknown or barely known. In 1876, when the German archaeologist Heinrich Schliemann undertook excavations in the cities of Troy and Mycenae, nothing was known of Greek history. The entire civilization we know as Mycenaean, mainly known through legendary Greek tales, was thus brought to light.

Beginning in 1900, the Englishman, Sir Arthur Evans, began to reveal the civilization of Crete.

Egypt itself was barely known through the testimony of Greek historians who only talked about the end of that great civilization. It has taken all the excavations of the past century and especially the deciphering of the hieroglyphs by the Frenchman, Jean-François Champoilion, to discover one of the most magnificent civilizations the world has ever known.

Elsewhere, certain civilizations which were also very important were only revealed through archaeological excavations. That is particularly the case of the Sumerians, who invented the basis of Western Civilization. It is also true of the Indus civilization, which developed along the banks of that river in Pakistan.

The classic Greek civilization left us texts and numerous objects of daily life, such as this beautiful box.

The discoverer of Troy, Heinrich Schliemann, excavated the circle of tombs in the palace of Mycenae in 1876.

17

Was Pompeii the first town to be excavated?

The state of excavations in Pompeii at the beginning of the nineteenth century.

The first excavations began in the fifteenth century in the ruins of Rome. The first buried town to be explored was Herculanum on the slopes of Vesuvius. Herculanum had been destroyed under the lava of that volcano at the same time as Pompeii during the eruption of A.D. 79. It was by chance, in 1710, that while digging a well, people found statues which came from the theater of the city. Nevertheless, the excavations were abandoned. It was too difficult to work in the lava that had hardened. Next, people became interested in a neighboring site located in a hill. Excavations began in 1748. Archaeologists soon realized that under this hill existed the entire town of Pompeii.

Presently, four-fifths of Pompeii has been uncovered, Herculanum only one-quarter.

Curiously, these discoveries did not encourage scientists of the eighteenth century to undertake other excavations. It wasn't until the nineteenth century that big archaeological works began in earnest. They started in 1842 with the excavations of Nineveh on the banks of the Tigris and with those in Mesopotamian sites.

1

2

3

1. Today, Pompeii has become a big tourist attraction. The city has again found a new life.

2. It is in Herculanum, another town hit by the eruption of A.D. 79, that the mosaic of Neptune and Amphitrite was found.

3-4. In the catastrophe of A.D. 79, numerous inhabitants of Pompeii were unable to flee. Imprints of their bodies in the ashes were molded by the archaeologists.

4

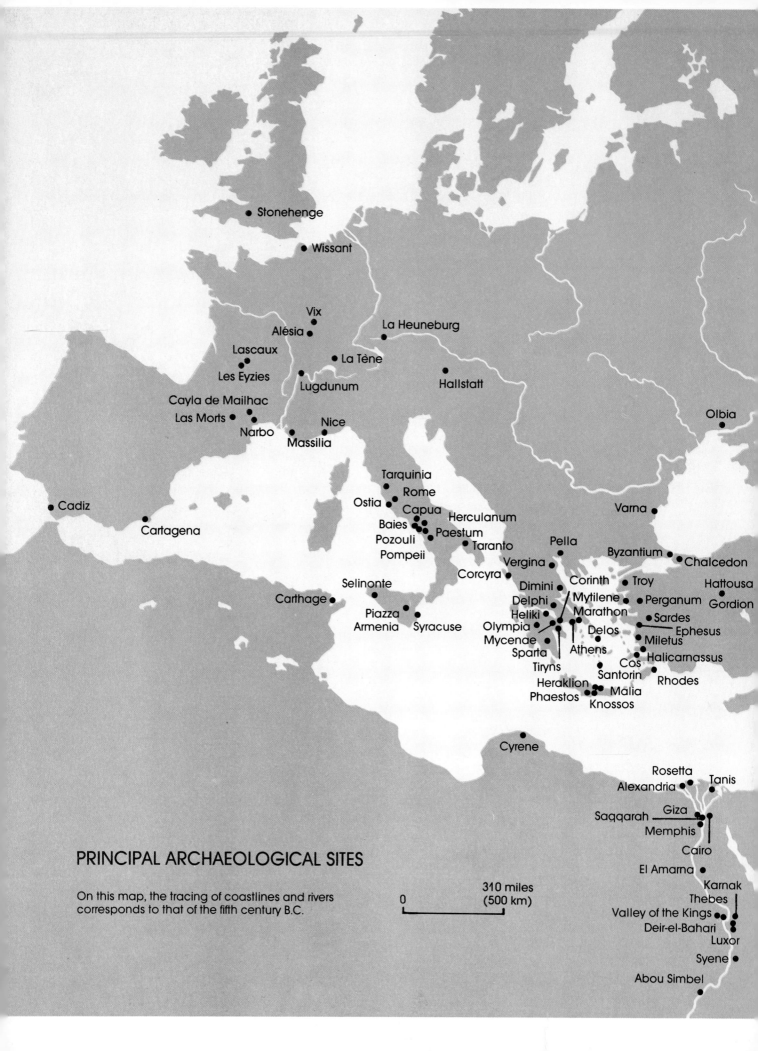

Stonehenge

Wissant

Vix
Alésia
Lascaux
Les Eyzies   La Tène   La Heuneburg
Cayla de Mailhac   Lugdunum
Las Morts   Hallstatt
Narbo   Nice
Massilia

Olbia

Cadiz
Cartagena

Tarquinia
Rome
Ostia
Capua   Herculanum   Varna
Baies   Paestum
Pozouli   Byzantium
Pompeii   Taranto   Chalcedon
               Pella
Selinonte   Corcyra   Vergina   Troy   Hattousa
                            Dimini Corinth   Perganum   Gordion
Carthage   Delphi Mytilene   Sardes
Piazza   Heliki Marathon   Ephesus
Armenia   Syracuse   Olympia   Delos   Miletus
                            Mycenae   Halicarnassus
                            Sparta   Athens   Cos
                            Tiryns   Santorin   Rhodes
                            Heraklion   Malia
                            Phaestos   Knossos

Cyrene

Rosetta
Tanis
Alexandria

Saqqarah   Giza
Memphis

Cairo

El Amarna

Karnak
Thebes
Valley of the Kings
Deir-el-Bahari
Luxor

Syene

Abou Simbel

PRINCIPAL ARCHAEOLOGICAL SITES

On this map, the tracing of coastlines and rivers
corresponds to that of the fifth century B.C.

0   310 miles
         (500 km)

Pazyryk

Tanaïs

Trebizond

Taxila

Harappa

Carchemish   Hatra   Nineveh
Ebla   Nimrod
Ugarit   Ashur   Ecbatana
Byblos   Mari
Sidon
Damascus   Babylon   Susa
Tyre   Mohenjo-Daro   Indus Valley
Jerusalem   Erech   Ur   Persepolis
Qumrân   Eridu   Nippur
Petra

A superb aerial photograph allows us to see at a glance the site of Ebla. At the right, you will see the excavation of the underground necropolis (cemetery) of that city: a new civilization recently brought to light.

Are there still civilizations and sites to be discovered?

Let's first define the word *civilization* as being an area of large-scale artistic, architectural, and urban creations. These achievements are the work of a population sharing the same laws and location, and the same political and religious rules. In that context, it seems as if all the great civilizations have been discovered.

Recently, however, the Italians discovered an ancient civilization about four thousand years old. In 1975, they exhumed thousands of tablets which revealed that they had just discovered a town called Ebla.

The city was the capital of a kingdom which extended over all the northern and eastern part of what is now Syria. A language closely resembling Hebrew was spoken there, and the tablets were easily deciphered.

Smaller sites which remain unknown are no doubt still very numerous. But there is not much hope of finding real lost cities, as was the case in 1946. That year, an American photographer, Giles G. Healey, happened to discover ruins of the village of Bonampak, belonging to the Mayan civilization.

THE ARCHAEOLOGIST

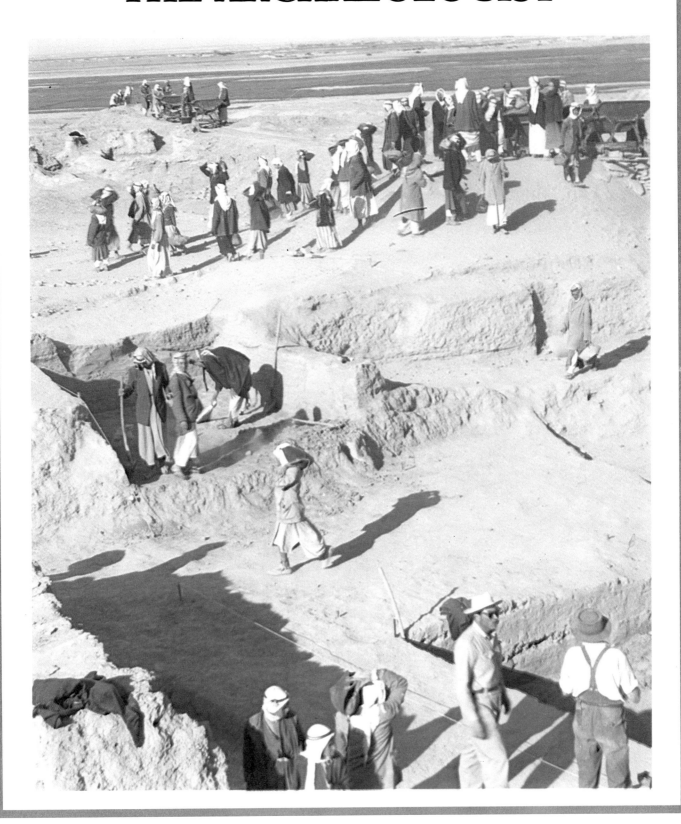

What is the difference between an archaeologist and a prehistorian?

The shelter under the Rock of the Magdalene, in Eyzies, is a good example of a prehistoric site. Here, prehistorians excavate very carefully, passing all the earth through a sieve. Before undertaking their research, they protect the site by erecting a roof, sometimes of sheet metal, so that the rain doesn't destroy the site.

For convenience sake, we have divided the "history" of humanity into two big periods, prehistory and historical periods. It is the beginning of writing which marks the difference. Thanks to writing, we know for certain the historic facts. From writing, we can actually know the thoughts of people, the reasons for their actions, and the laws which govern them. By contrast, the objects found in prehistoric sites remain unclear.

The prehistorian is an archaeologist who studies the periods preceding the appearance of writing. Other archaeologists specialize in one particular civilization or another. Egyptologists study Egypt, Hellenists study Greece, Latinists Rome, Assyriologists Assyria, and so on.

Methods of excavation are not the same. In general, prehistorians only explore very select sites where the slightest object, even a grain of pollen, must be gathered and kept. However, large archaeological sites like Babylon or Nineveh make it impossible to proceed with such great attention to detail.

How far back can the first archaeological research be traced?

In the middle of the last century, archaeological exploration began to develop. The discoverers were often content with marking the monuments and only partially uncovering them. That is what Stephens and Catherwood did in the Mayan country in Mexico. Here the two explorer/archaeologists are shown with their entourage in the site of Tulum in the Yucatan.

That all depends on the meaning of the term *archaeological research*. Does it mean finding ancient objects to collect or even to reproduce in a modern way? In that case, you could say that research goes back for centuries. In fact, the last kings of Babylon, especially Nabonid in the sixth century B.C., collected sacred objects from temples. The Romans searched for objects of art made by the Greeks, which they often had artists of the time imitate.

But if *archaeological research* means excavations conducted in a scientific manner, you could say that the first date back to the 1920s. Certain contemporary archaeologists even estimate that true scientific works only go back about twenty years.

In general, archaeological research truly developed toward the middle of the nineteenth century. It was during that time that excavations multiplied across the whole world and that the first prehistoric research began.

Who are the most famous archaeologists?

With a theatrical gesture, Jacques de Morgan presents a golden crown to the crowd—a find which he had just made in the tomb of an Egyptian princess.

In this field, as in many others, fame is not always the best description. The most famous archaeologists were, above all, pioneers because the territory they worked was new and their finds always interesting.

Boucher de Perthes was considered the "father" of prehistory in the middle of the last century. Already mentioned are Botta and Layard in the area of Assyriology. Now add Ernest de Sarzec, who discovered the Sumerians; the German Hugo Winckler, who, at the beginning of this century, revealed the Hittites; the Englishman Sir John Marshall, who was the first, in 1921, to excavate Harappa, one of the principal sites of the Indus civilization.

In Egypt, hieroglyphics were deciphered by the Frenchman Champollion and his compatriot Auguste Mariette, in the middle of the eighteenth century.

At the beginning of this century, Jacques de Morgan, a geologist, distinguished himself with his archaeological work as much in Egypt as in Iran where he undertook excavations on the gigantic site of Suse.

Also remarkable are Heinrich Schliemann and Sir Arthur Evans. Above all, in the twentieth century, is Abbott Breuil, considered by some to be the "pope" of prehistory. He discovered the Lascaux grotto in the Dordogne region of France.

The overthrow of Troy as seen by a painter of the seventeenth century. In the center is the famous wooden horse built by the Greeks.

How did Heinrich Schliemann become an archaeologist?

Heinrich Schliemann, standing before an attentive audience in London, talks about the results of his discoveries at Troy and Mycenae.

Heinrich Schliemann's life was outstanding. The son of a German pastor, he was born in 1822. He was eight years old when he saw an engraving representing the overthrow of Troy. He promised himself then that he would find this city which archaeologists thought was a legend.

At age fourteen, he boarded a ship in Hamburg, but it was wrecked on the coast of Holland. He found himself completely destitute in a foreign country. He lived there in poverty, learned several languages (among them Russian), and then started working in a business which sent him to Russia.

Between 1846-1868 in Russia, he acquired an immense fortune which permitted him to devote his time to his childhood dream.

In 1870, he found himself in Turkey. There he dug up a large Asian Turkish mound near the Dardanelles—the Hissarlik Tell. In 1871, he undertook the excavation of the site with his own funds.

We are now certain that the city Schliemann excavated is the city of Troy of which the poet Homer spoke in the *Iliad* and the *Odyssey*.

Elsewhere, always at his expense, Schliemann excavated the ruins of Mycenae and Tirynth in Greece. He thus brought to light two of the principal sites of the civilization which ruled in Greece from 1600 to 1200 B.C., and which is called the Mycenaean civilization.

How did Arthur John Evans find the Cretan civilization?

After having found the palace of Knossos, Arthur John Evans tried to partially reconstruct it. Other scientists tried to make accurate reconstructions on paper, like this one of the so-called Dolphin's Room.

In the history of Greece, Mycenae and Troy were legendary cities. This was also the case with Knossos, on the island of Crete, discovered in the nineteenth century. Schliemann had already had the idea of exploring this site. He had given up the idea because of conditions imposed by the owners of that region.

Then Arthur John Evans appeared. Born in 1851, he had distinguished himself already by his archaeological research in England.

Without revealing his goal, Evans started to acquire, little by little, the lands on which lay the village of Knossos, next to the port of Candie.

In 1900, as owner of most of the lands, he began his first campaign of excavations, assisted by the director of the English school of archaeology in Athens. From his first works, he uncovered a series of rooms—the shops of the royal palace of the city. Evans pursued his exploration until 1914, uncovering the whole of the vast palace constructed around a large rectangular-shaped courtyard.

Work was interrupted during World War I and started again as soon as the war was over. It continued until 1935. In that year, Sir Arthur John Evans retired. He was eighty-four years old and died six years later.

At the same time Evans' research was going on, other palaces were dug up in Crete. Work was being done in Phaistos by the Italians and in Mallia by the French. Thus, the testimonies of a brilliant civilization, of which even the Greeks themselves had forgotten, were revealed.

Archaeology today involves very meticulous teamwork.

How does a person become an archaeologist today?

The first quality of an archaeologist is passion, the profound desire to know the lives of people who lived in the past. This passion often develops in childhood. Henry Schliemann was only eight years old when he decided to find the ruins of Troy. It can come much later in life, however. Jean-Frederique de Waldeck, for example, had a brilliant military career and fought under Napoleon. He was sixty-six years old when he discovered his desire to become an archaeological explorer. He went off in search of the Mayas in the forests of Mexico.

To become an archaeologist, it is important that you have an education. A taste for art history and dead languages such as Latin is also necessary.

Nevertheless, those who cannot or do not want to engage in a long course of study always find a way to participate as amateurs on excavation sites. There are even official digs where, after a time, you can obtain a certificate of aptitude.

Archaeology of yesterday required that archaeologists also be explorers, like Charnay, shown here in the Mexican forest.

1. Prospecting with a magnetometer

2. Sighting

5. Photography

6. Registering discoveries

How do archaeologists excavate?

Over the excavation, string delineates squares. Archaeologists can thus map out the exact area where each find is made.

Archaeological excavations call for precise techniques, which are learned in books and especially on actual sites. In detail, these techniques may vary from one site to another: a prehistoric cave, a buried town, remains of a small dwelling, a tomb, etc.

First of all, the site must be divided into small square segments with string or simply traced on the ground. This gridwork, drawn on a map, then allows identification of the exact place where objects have been found.

If this grid shows the surface location, it must also be able to show where objects are deeper down. That is why archaeologists work in relatively thin layers. These layers follow archaeological levels. Excavation by levels is also called "stratigraphical" excavation.

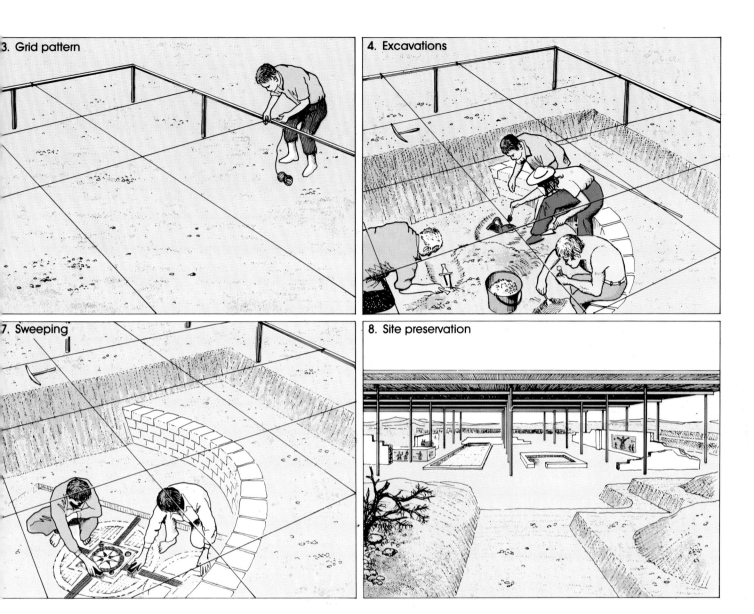

3. Grid pattern

4. Excavations

7. Sweeping

8. Site preservation

Must a person be very educated in order to direct an excavation?

The supervision of a dig, even a small one, always requires a high level of skill and education.

First, of course, the archaeologist must possess techniques used in modern excavations. In addition, he or she must be able to identify with certainty all the objects found—coins, pottery, and so on.

A good archaeologist possesses a solid knowledge of historical, cultural, and social events which characterize the civilization he or she is researching.

When are excavations carried out?

This burial mound in France is called Caesar's Fort. It has not yet been excavated.

Excavations can last from several weeks to several months. The planning of these digs remains variable depending on the regions which are being explored. In America, excavations usually take place in summer, lasting sometimes until autumn. Good weather is indispensable because the elements can hinder the work.

In tropical countries, work can only be done during the dry seasons which vary depending on the region. In the Orient, where summer is very hot, springtime or autumn are the preferred excavation times. Schliemann wanted to explore the city of Troy during the month of December. The result—icy winds coming from the Black Sea, which considerably hindered his work.

Thus, in any country, with the possible exception of the Sahara, winter is not a favorable time to undertake a dig. Nevertheless, the Germans who excavated Babylon worked without interruption, winter and summer, for many years.

Are there still many sites remaining to be excavated?

Another burial mound covers the reputed tomb of Midas in central Turkey. A burial chamber twenty-eight centuries old was found there.

In spite of the thoughtless destruction of numerous sites by the undertaking of public works and construction of skyscrapers, there is still enough work to last for centuries!

There is not one site or one city, even a small one, which has been entirely excavated. In Mesopotamia alone, several thousand sites have been located, but only a few hundred have been explored.

There are large burial mounds of earth which hide important constructions or tombs. But there are also hundreds of thousands of sites of less importance, completely buried, whose existence we don't even know about. Research, called prospecting, especially with aerial photography, reveals new sites every day.

These bone toys and dice are from the Roman era.

Can people collect archaeological objects?

There are two means of obtaining archaeological pieces—by excavating or by purchasing them. However, the majority of archaeologists deposit their finds in museums.

In some cities, merchants sell archaeological pieces which generally come from excavations which took place in other countries in past centuries.

People who travel, especially in Mediterranean countries, can obtain archaeological items, often at very high prices. Usually the pieces are fakes or they may have been acquired illegally.

These fragments of pottery bear the names of people the Athenians wanted to banish from the city. They date back to the fifth century B.C.

How did Champollion decipher hieroglyphics?

In deciphering hieroglyphics, Champollion interpreted ancient Egyptian texts.

In 1798, French troops under Napoleon invaded Egypt. But the invasion was not entirely military. French scientists are seen here studying the Sphinx at Giza.

The term *hieroglyphics* designates the drawings which make up ancient Egyptian writing. The Egyptians knew how to write in hieroglyphics even after Roman and Greek domination, but the ancient authors did not leave the secret of this writing.

For centuries, European scholars pondered these mysterious signs without being able to understand them. It was not only a question of finding some letters of our alphabet which corresponded to the drawings but also of understanding what they meant in their language.

This task was the work of Jean-François Champollion. This French scholar, born in Figeac in 1790, was fortunate to have been able to study a stone on which some texts were inscribed. One in Greek went back to the second century B.C. Another text was written in hieroglyphics. Champollion discovered that the text in hieroglyphics was the translation of the Greek text.

Champollion then began to compare the Greek letters and the hieroglyphics. By studying the comparisons as though he were deciphering a code, he was able to transcribe a portion of the hieroglyphics. Once this work was done, he recognized the language in which the Egyptian text was written. It was an ancestor of Coptic, the language of Egyptian Christians.

This stone, which was the secret of hieroglyphics, had been found in Rosetta, Egypt, in the eighteenth century. It is called the *Rosetta Stone.*

The Rosetta Stone.

The Battle of the Pyramids (pictured in the distance) pitted French troops against Muslim troops.

How can totally unknown writing be deciphered?

The methods vary according to the writing and the language. Researchers are often able to decipher very ancient texts by starting with more modern languages and working their way back in time bit by bit. Thanks to cuneiform writing (wedge-shaped writing) from Persia in the sixth century B.C., researchers were able to find the meaning of Mesopotamian cuneiform.

The translation of writing found on the tablets discovered at various sites in Greece was more difficult. This writing, known as *linear,* resisted all research. There was no existing bilingual text as had been the case with the Rosetta Stone used by Champollion.

Early in the 1950s, a young English cryptographer, Michael G.F. Ventris, invented an ingenious system of grids. He was inspired by methods used by counter-espionage offices to decipher secret codes. He finally discovered that the language spoken by the inhabitants of Greece and Crete, fourteen centuries B.C., was already . . . Greek.

This text written with cuneiform signs on a "prism" in terra-cotta dates to the seventh century B.C.

Are there still undeciphered languages?

Egyptian hieroglyphics on a scroll.

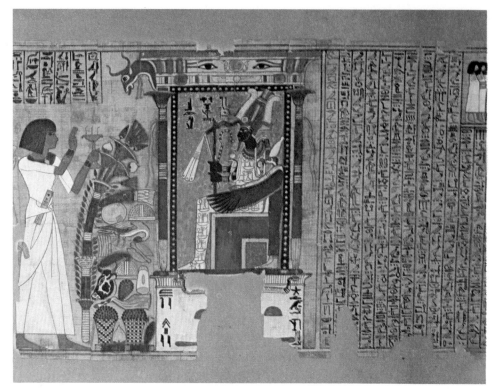

A still-undeciphered writing—Mayan signs on a manuscript board of the fifteenth century.

Papyrus scroll is often found in a very damaged condition. It is a challenging puzzle to reconstruct.

Yes, there are undeciphered languages even today. One example is the *linear* writing of Greece. This writing, which is really called *linear B,* is derived from another writing called *linear A.* Linear A was only utilized on the island of Crete. Several signs from A are found in B. But others are peculiar to A and cannot be compared to anything else. That is why linear A remains an unknown language. The words formed by its signs are not understood. It is an ancient language of Crete, no doubt.

Another mysterious language is Etruscan. It can be deciphered because it is written in an alphabet resembling the ancient alphabets of Italy and Greece. But the language cannot be understood as read.

We know of other languages which we can't read either. In the Indus Valley, for example, small stone and clay emblems have been found. On them are signs in an undeciphered language. By contrast, we do know the spoken language of the Mayas which is still used by certain populations of Central America.

THE WORK OF
ARCHAEOLOGISTS

How do archaeologists recognize a site to be excavated?

This aerial photograph shows the outline of a villa of the Roman era. The map marks the area clearly, even before the excavations have begun. Such photographs greatly facilitate the work of archaeologists.

That is what archaeologists call prospecting.

It is easy to locate ruins made of stone because their presence on the landscape is very obvious.

In the East, the plains are littered with burial sites called *tells*. These sites rise into the air in the form of hills or mounds.

Research becomes complicated when the site is buried deeply in the ground, which is often the case in Europe. In that case, there are several ways of locating it. For example, certain roads in the countryside lead nowhere. In general, these roads end at a site. Sometimes, fragments of pottery cover the ground, confirming this hypothesis. The pres-

ence of a Roman site is often signaled by materials (sculpted stones or stones bearing inscriptions) which were reused in the construction of local houses and churches.

Aerial photography is also an excellent means of detecting a site buried in the earth.

Aerial photography

Aerial photography was invented by the English and French after World War I. Aerial photography involves photographing the earth from an airplane. Buried walls and other secluded sections of a site can easily be located thanks to the contrast in colors.

Can a person excavate a site alone?

It has been done in the past and can still be done. Usually the site is small because an excavation requires long and meticulous work. But, if a person is dedicated to putting in the necessary time, he or she can accomplish quite a bit alone or with a couple of assistants.

Abbot Jean Durand was a grocer before becoming a priest. About thirty years ago, he undertook some remarkable prehistoric excavations by himself in Ariege, France, particularly in the cave of Las Morts.

Odette Taffanel and her brother, Jean, are better known. Beginning in 1939, they excavated the area of Cayla de Mailhac in the Aude region of France by themselves. They discovered tombs and construction dating back to the Iron Age. These two dedicated researchers were of peasant origins, but they knew their work as well as if they were archaeologists with college degrees.

Here is what the personal property of a tomb looks like at the moment it is discovered. This pottery was buried in the ground in the seventh century B.C.

Is an excavation very expensive?

An amateur only needs the price of tools and instruments. The costs remain low.

However, when it is a matter of a large site with many workers, technicians, and numerous archaeologists and specialists, excavations can cost a small fortune.

In archaeology, there is work to be done at all prices and for all budgets.

Who donates the money to finance an excavation?

There, too, the possibilities are numerous. Small amateur digs are financed by the excavators themselves. In many parts of the world, excavations are financed by the government. In the United States, excavations are often sponsored by large universities. Sometimes, wealthy private individuals finance certain digs which interest them.

Pictured is a very large archaeological site in Mesopotamia. Andre Parrot recruited about two hundred men on the spot to dig and remove the earth. Work on a site this vast is very different from work on a small plot.

Are many people usually required on an excavation?

The number of workers at a site is variable. In sites where only amateurs or students work, the excavators are not very specialized except for the director of the dig and one or two assistants. Each of them uses the spade and pickax but must also be capable of undertaking more delicate operations. The finds must be cataloged, reported on a map, labeled, and so on. At an average-size dig, the number of excavators can vary between ten and twenty.

On large excavations, the organization is more complicated. Some are distinguished as staff or technicians; others are workers. The staff generally consists of the director of the excavation, one or more assistants, an architect in charge of studying and reconstructing the maps of monuments, and a photographer who documents the digs and the objects found. Some digs add a numismatist (a specialist in coins) and an epigraphist, who deciphers any texts found.

In digs at Mari, Mesopotamia, Andre Parrot hired more than two hundred men. That is an uncommonly high number.

What tools do archaeologists use?

An excavation requires many different materials. For mapmaking, a special compass which measures the incline of slopes, a surveyor's decameter, a double ruler, and geometry instruments are needed.

For tracing maps on paper, squares, a compass, rulers, and graph paper are needed.

The tools of an excavation are the spade, the pickax, and a certain number of small instruments—coal spades, trowels, scrapers, small picks, knives, needles, brushes, and tweezers. The earth is removed with the aid of wheelbarrows or baskets, but it first goes through sieves.

From pickax to tweezers, archaeologists use many tools.

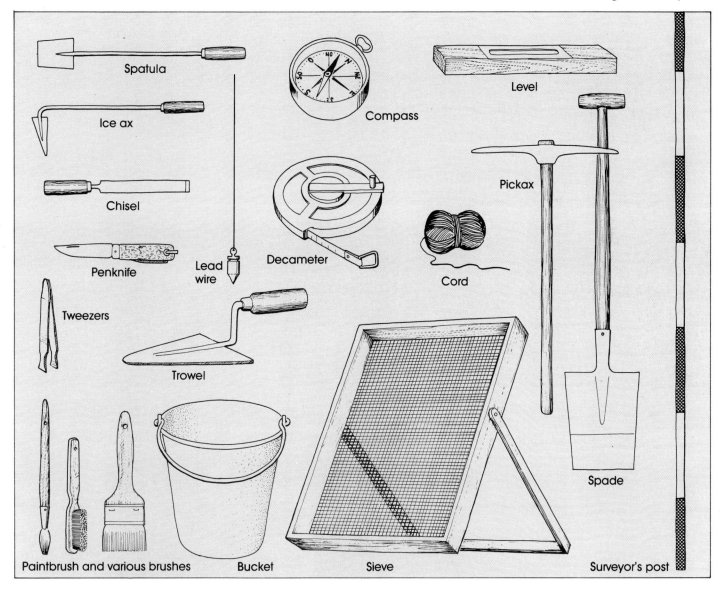

Spatula

Ice ax

Chisel

Penknife

Lead wire

Tweezers

Trowel

Paintbrush and various brushes

Bucket

Sieve

Compass

Decameter

Cord

Level

Pickax

Spade

Surveyor's post

Do archaeologists work under the water?

Yes, and it is becoming more and more frequent. It is what is called underwater archaeology. It has been known for a long time that parts of ancient cities were buried under the sea. Many old vessels also have sunk with their cargoes.

During the last twenty years, the technique of underwater excavation has been perfected. Much the same instruments are used as on land digs. The grids which divide the site into squares should be made of rigid metal, however. Small spades are also used to find and gather objects. Mud is removed from the dig with a long tube which sucks up the mud and spits it out at the surface. These methods have enabled archaeologists to excavate numerous wrecks of old Roman, Greek, and Phoenician ships and the submerged parts of ancient cities.

Pictured is a specialized ship equipped for underwater excavation.

Even under the water, archaeologists draw up a grid and number the objects, but underwater excavation is slow and difficult.

What are the objects found most often?

Obviously, the objects vary accordingly to the site, region, and time. Almost all the sites from the neolithic age (latest period of the Stone Age) have pottery buried in them.

This pottery represents the basic domestic life of all dwellings. It was the equivalent of china, earthenware, or the plastic materials that we use today.

Because pottery is fragile, archaeologists usually only discover fragments. But pottery differs depending on the region and the era so even fragments offer researchers a host of very precise clues. Thanks to pieces of pottery, the archaeologist will often be able to date a site. He or she may also be able to determine the lifestyle of the people who occupied it, their relations among themselves, the type of activities they practiced, their food, and much more. In tombs, pottery which is found intact is considered art.

From the fourth century B.C. in Greece and Italy and then in the Greek/Roman world, coins became increasingly used. These are also exceptional testimonies to life in times gone by.

Another object often brought to light in western European sites from the Iron Age (1200 B.C.) is a sort of hook in the shape of a safety pin, which was used to keep draped clothes on the body.

Other treasures found at digs include statues of stone, bronze, and clay, dishes often in silver, iron tools, keys, jewels, cloth, and wooden or vegetable fiber objects.

A cache of pottery from 1500 B.C. in a tomb on the island of Santorin in Greece.

This bronze lion was discovered in Mari, Mesopotamia.

Who gets the objects that are found?

That all depends on the laws of the countries and the agreements signed by the director of the excavation and the official authorities. In most countries, the state is the owner of all found objects. The objects can be seen by the public in museums.

Some countries like France or Belgium accord half of the find to the discoverer, the other half to the owner of the land. However, archaeologists often have an understanding with the owners that they will lease the property and keep all the finds themselves.

People who organize their own digs keep any found objects but often open small, private museums.

Finally, when archaeologists of a western nation make excavations in a Third World country (Middle East, Africa, or Latin America), the host countries keep the ownership of the finds, but they do accord a certain number of pieces to the country which organized the dig.

In what condition are objects usually found?

When excavating a house, fragile objects (pottery and glass) are usually found damaged, often in thousands of pieces. Sometimes pottery can be reglued, at least in part, which makes it possible to reconstruct the object.

Bronze coins are often tarnished, but they can be cleaned up and returned to their original appearance. Iron is generally covered with a thick layer of rust which is much more difficult to remove.

Stone statues are sometimes well preserved, although certain parts may be broken.

The most beautiful and best preserved objects are in tombs. When a tomb is made up of a chamber with a roof that is not crumbled, the contents remain intact. That is how many magnificent Greek vases have been saved. A great number of them come from the tombs of Etruria, mostly opened in the nineteenth century.

Gold objects are almost always intact. But bronze or silver vases must undergo treatment before regaining their original shape and shine.

An archaeologist loosens an alignment of two thousand-year-old sculpted wood in France.

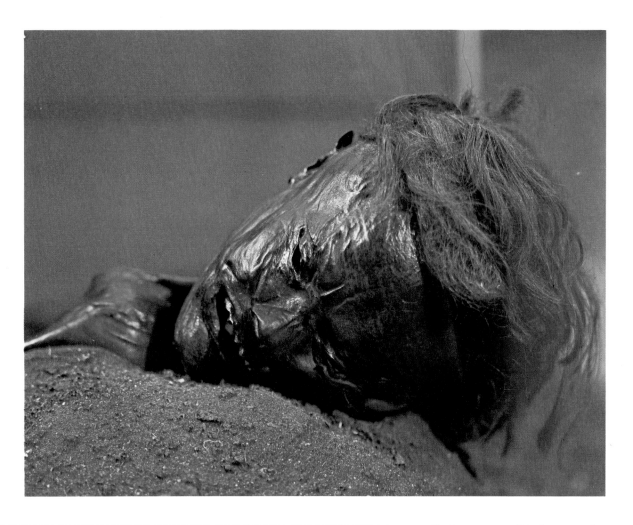

How long have fragile or perishable objects been preserved?

Peat was responsible for preserving the mummy of this man, found in the swamps of Grauballe in Denmark.

As a general rule, glass, furniture, all wooden items, cloth, and carpeting are only preserved for a few centuries. All tombs discovered so far have been exposed to humidity or bad weather. The elements decompose most objects.

However, some exceptional conditions have preserved a certain number of ancient works which might have rapidly disappeared. Near certain springs, sanctuaries have been found. Wooden statues have been preserved in stagnant water.

At the site of Pazyryk in Siberia, infiltrations of water turned into ice. It is that ice which preserved felt carpets and the entire tatooed skin of a man buried in a tomb 2,500 years ago.

In very dry and desert regions, things are preserved fairly well. The extreme dryness of the air in Egypt protected not only the paintings which covered the walls of tombs but also more fragile objects—cloth, sandals of raffia or papyrus, papyrus leaves on which texts were made, cords, wigs, wooden furniture, and even mummified bodies.

It is ice which preserved the contents of the tomb of Pazyryk in Siberia. Without it, this horseman, represented on a piece of felt, would not have survived to modern times.

The Swedes succeeded well in retrieving the *Gustave Wasa* from the water. But preserving a wooden boat of this size in the open air poses many problems.

Modern technology makes the preservation of this mummified body possible.

How are fragile objects preserved after their discovery?

All objects must be carefully treated once they have been removed from the ground. Generally, pottery is simply brushed or washed, but it may be coated with a thin layer of transparent plastic. Coins are cleaned with chemical and electric products to preserve them.

Iron objects are more delicate. When the layer of rust is too thick, the object's exterior is treated in a laboratory. But often the interior continues to deteriorate.

Even more difficult is the preservation of wooden objects found in humid environments. The Swedes have become the great specialists of this technique. They worked hard after the underwater discovery of an entire warship, the *Gustave Wasa,* dating from the seventeenth century.

The wood must be maintained for a certain period of time in the humid environment, otherwise it will dry out too quickly, contract and become warped, or even crumble into dust. Wooden objects must undergo a long and extremely complicated chemical treatment.

There is a great risk when Egyptian mummies are placed in a museum. They are attacked by microbes which threaten to decompose them. In order to avoid that catastrophe, mummies are treated by modern techniques of preservation.

The mummy of Ramses II was recently treated by French technicians. It had been attacked by microorganisms and was in danger of completely decomposing.

The mummy of Ramses II in its wooden coffin. The pharaoh died more than three thousand years ago.

Museums do not have to be sad and somber. The museum of Cologne, Germany, is a good example with its beautiful galleries and exciting exhibits. Shown here is a mausoleum of the Roman era.

What is a museum?

It is a building designed to gather and preserve masterpieces of art and artifacts. The first museum was founded in Alexandria, Egypt, in the third century B.C.

Modern museums display relics from the past so that everyone can examine them. In archaeological museums, there are laboratories where people study these works scientifically.

There are several types of archaeological museums. First, there are the great national museums like the Louvre in Paris. Regional museums are often more specialized, with some entirely devoted to archaeology. Finally, the third type of archaeological museum is one which is attached to an important site or to several sites in an area. It holds all the finds coming from those sites.

How are objects dated?

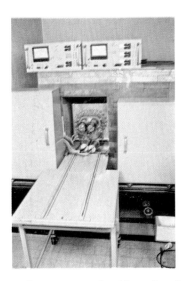

In this oven, certain objects found by archaeologists undergo the method of dating by carbon 14.

Archaeologists work layer by layer, level by level. If they can date an object found in any given layer, they will also know the age of other objects in the same layer. Thus, coins, especially Greek or Roman ones, make it possible to date the layer within a few years.

Inscriptions and tablets bearing the names of people with known dates of birth and death render a similar service.

People have also discovered known and dated objects in sites far removed from their original area. These discoveries are full of infor-mation. Because objects do not travel by themselves, commercial ex-changes must have existed between one particular region and another.

Sometimes, in order to date their finds, archaeologists call upon special-ized laboratories. That is how dat-ing by the carbon 14 method came into existence. Carbon 14, contained in materials of biological origin (bones, wood, etc.), has the peculi-arity of transforming over time. The laboratory's task is, therefore, to determine the approximate stage of this transformation.

Can people reconstruct ruins of monuments?

The Door of Ishtar was reconstructed at the exact entrance of the excavations of Babylon. The enameled bricks shine brilliantly in the sun.

Reconstruction of ancient mon-uments is often a case of simply re-erecting columns of temples bat-tered by time, men, or most often earthquakes. That was done for cer-tain temples in Sicily and Greece, in particular the temple of Athena Nike on the Acropolis of Athens. When ancient material is missing, new materials can be used to complete the missing pieces of architecture. Arthur Evans rebuilt part of the palace of Knossos in Crete in this way with concrete.

There are some remarkable ex-amples of reconstruction. First, there is the Stoa of Attale on the Agora of Athens. That was a portico used as a market or offices in Greece. It was entirely rebuilt by Americans who employed an architect special-izing in archaeology.

Americans also rebuilt a monu-mental gymnasium and a large syn-agogue in Sardes in Asia Minor.

In Ephesus in Asia Minor, the Aus-trians remarkably reconstructed the facade of columns of a library from the Roman era.

Yet such work is very costly and is only rarely attempted.

Are discoveries of modern science used in archaeology?

They are, more and more. Sometimes, however, there is the problem of needing equipment which is still too costly for certain archaeological digs.

For prospecting, aerial photography is used. Electric energy also enters into an operation. A method called catalysis is used to clean bronze coins. "Sounding" floors with electricity also helps to find buried walls.

Another instrument detects magnetism which is still emitted by clay or metal objects. Even if these objects are deeply buried in the earth, this apparatus makes it possible to find them.

Chemical analysis of metals and pottery is also very useful. It informs researchers of the actual composition of certain objects, the way in which they were made, and even the geographic origin of the basic materials used.

Ultraviolet or infrared photography also gives precise information about the composition of objects and methods of manufacture.

Thermoluminescence is a technique used to determine the dates of origin of pottery, tiles, and clay artifacts.

These two drawings explain how biological matter can be dated by the method of carbon 14 (left) or by dendrochronology (right).

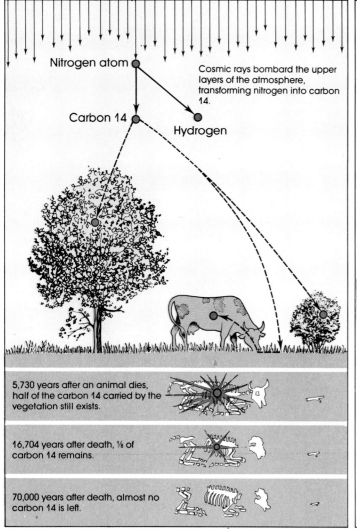

Nitrogen atom

Cosmic rays bombard the upper layers of the atmosphere, transforming nitrogen into carbon 14.

Carbon 14

Hydrogen

5,730 years after an animal dies, half of the carbon 14 carried by the vegetation still exists.

16,704 years after death, ⅛ of carbon 14 remains.

70,000 years after death, almost no carbon 14 is left.

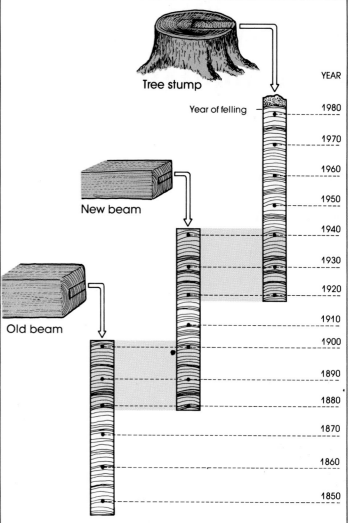

Tree stump

Year of felling

New beam

Old beam

YEAR

1980
1970
1960
1950
1940
1930
1920
1910
1900
1890
1880
1870
1860
1850

LIFE IN ANCIENT TIMES

Why were treasures put in tombs?

A bull's head in gold decorates the harp discovered in the tomb of Queen Puabi.

This drawing shows a reconstruction of the funeral of a Sumerian queen who lived about 4,500 years ago.

Most people believe that there is another life after death. They respect the idea that the soul is eternal.

Ancient people, and even many people in the world today, believed that life after death is similar to that on earth. They believed that the dead had the same needs as the living, that they needed to eat and drink and to amuse themselves and even work. That is why people placed objects in the tombs. They wanted to make the dead person's life pleasant in the hereafter.

In certain eras, the wives and servants of powerful men accompanied them to their tombs. These unfortunate ones were sacrificed. They were found in certain burial chambers like those of Ur in Mesopotamia and various Chinese tombs. Animals were sacrificed even more frequently.

Ancient Egyptians are depicted gathering papyrus.

Did people write on paper?

Paper was unknown in ancient times. It was invented by the Chinese, who made it from silk rags during the first few centuries A.D.

In the eighth century, paper was introduced in the West by the Arabs who knew of it from the Chinese in central Asia.

The Egyptians wrote on papyrus. This plant grew in abundance in the Nile Valley. Its stem could be unrolled so as to form fine vegetable strips which were glued together to form long scrolls. Greeks and Romans inherited this technique from the Egyptians. Their books were also made up of rolls of papyrus. They also wrote on wooden tablets coated with wax. The writing could be erased by spreading a new coat of wax on the surface.

The Greeks, for their part, invented a material made of finely-tailored skins cut into leaves. It was called parchment.

As for the people of the Near East, they wrote with the aid of hard points on tablets of raw clay. The clay had to be hollowed out with the point of a reed. Only simple characters were possible, and that is how cuneiform writing came about.

This young Roman, found in Pompeii, writes with a "stylet" on wooden tablets coated in wax.

Were there schools?

A Roman teacher and his pupils with a parchment scroll.

As a society perfects itself and evolves, it creates schools where this knowledge is passed on. For example, at the same time that writing was developing in the kingdom of Sumer in the south of today's Iraq, schools were being organized.

Excavations have helped us discover that in palaces, rooms furnished with clay benches look like they were used as classrooms for students. From the complexities of cuneiform writings, hieroglyphics, grammar, religious legends, and the law, it is easy to determine that students of ancient times had long hours of studying to do.

Just as in Mesopotamia and all the Near East, Egyptian children went to schools called "houses of life," which were also tied in to the temples.

In Greece and Rome, children went to school from the time they were little. Learning was directed by scholars who taught philosophy, law, and speech (rhetoric). These studies were carried out until the student was in his or her twenties.

Did children have toys?

Some very ancient toys have been discovered. In the Indus Valley, small miniature clay chariots have been found. These strongly resemble wagons with wheels which are still used today.

In Egypt and especially in Greece, toys were discovered in children's burial chambers. They are mostly dolls either of rags, wood, or clay. The clay dolls are often statuettes with moving arms. There were also small models of animals, wooden horses on wheels, hippopotami with moving lower jaws, geese, lions, pigs, and so on.

Some clay artifacts represent groups—women gathered working together or occupied with various tasks. In that case, it is still not known if they are toys or scale models, depicting life in ancient times.

The ancient Greeks played with yo-yos, kites, and tops.

This small clay chariot comes from Mesopotamia. It was a child's toy several thousand years ago.

The three people in this Roman mosaic are playing with dice.

This Egyptian queen moves pieces on a board game.

What were the games they played?

Two children spin a top. This sculpture, which is more than three thousand years old, was found in Karkemish in eastern Turkey.

There were children's games and adult games. Some were played by both children and adults.

Boys played war and fighting games. Girls played with dolls and balls.

Most of the games we know are shown in paintings or other artwork. Some of the objects themselves have also been discovered. The games of "knucklebones" and dice were particularly loved by the Greeks and Romans.

A certain Greek game—"cottabe" —consisted, usually on the occasion of a banquet, of throwing the last drops of wine in a cup to a pre-cise point in the room.

There were also numerous ball games in ancient times. One of the most unusual is Egyptian—the players tossed balls from their positions upon the backs of their partners.

The Egyptians played many games. One of them, the "snake," was played with a plaque shaped like a coiled snake. A complete game has been found consisting of a small table pierced with holes in which players placed small batons decorated with the head of a dog or jackal. Found in the royal tombs of Ur were checkerboards more than forty-five centuries old.

Did people partake in leisure activities?

People in ancient times did not devote their entire lives to working. In certain civilizations, one day a week, the Sabbath, was a holiday. During the course of the year, there were many festival times when people celebrated.

These festivals were even more numerous in countries where people worshiped several gods. In Greece, during certain periods, there were more holidays than workdays.

Not everyone worked in those times. In Greece, many citizens possessed enough land to be able to live off its profits. Their enterprises were often maintained by slaves.

Rome invented a unique system beginning in the first century A.D. Numerous citizens attached themselves to wealthy people. Every day they paid them a visit and complimented them. In return, they received food for the day.

A great portion of the inhabitants of Rome, in those days, did not work. The state supported all these individuals. Ships filled with grain arrived from North Africa and Egypt to feed everyone.

A diver is shown in a painting from a Greek tomb.

Did people hunt and fish for pleasure?

In prehistory, hunting and fishing were part of vital daily activities. It was the only means for people to feed themselves.

But when towns grew up and societies organized themselves, hunting and fishing became leisure activities.

In Egypt and the Orient, kings and nobles hunted for enjoyment with spears and bows. They even sought out animals that were dangerous, like the lion or the wild bull, because hunting was a sport and an exercise which prepared men for war. These hunts were conducted with chariots, and later, on horseback. They also hunted birds, especially in Egypt, with nets or boomerangs.

The Greeks loved hunting and practiced it like a sport. They hunted all sorts of game from the boar to the hare. They hunted on foot or horseback and with dogs.

Prehistoric people also fished with lines and nets in the sea, rivers, and lakes.

These two Roman mosaics depict two sports widely practiced in ancient times. Fishermen (bottom) used equipment similar to the equipment used today—lines, hooks, landing nets, and fishing nets. By contrast, hunting (top) has evolved quite a lot. Without firearms, hunting required serious training with a spear or bow. It was a very dangerous sport.

How were houses built?

In the eighteenth century, explorers found an immense Roman villa by digging tunnels under the modern villa of Portici. Statues and other objects were uncovered, and the original design of the villa was revealed. The villa is still buried. But recently, the wealthy American, Paul Getty, built a house in California modeled after it. Pictured are two views of this modern-day Roman villa.

In ancient times, the shapes and makeup of houses varied a lot from one civilization to another. Today, there are still enormous differences all over the world in the traditional dwellings of certain cultures.

In Pakistan, the houses surrounded a small interior courtyard onto which ground floor rooms opened. A staircase ran to other floors from that courtyard. This type of construction can be found today in southern Spain. Interior courtyards were called *patios*.

Certain Greek houses fronted the street with a small courtyard or garden, similar to some of today's suburban homes.

In Egypt, the houses of the wealthy were surrounded by gardens. In the back were grain barns, farmyards, and so on.

The characteristic house of Pompeii partially imitated Greek houses of the third and second centuries B.C. The bedrooms surrounded a large chamber whose ceiling was open. This chamber was called the *atrium* and was used as a living room. Toward the rear of the building were gardens and porches surrounded also by living rooms.

Were there any highrise buildings?

This model gives an idea of what could have been a house occupied by several tenants in Rome.

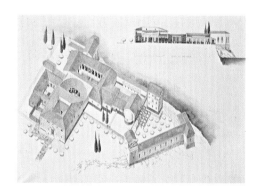

Wealthy Romans had vast houses in the country. Pictured is a house that belonged to a Roman lawyer, Pliny. It was situated at the edge of the sea.

In most ancient civilizations, houses were for single family units. The inhabitants were generally the owners. In the countryside, houses were built by the people who lived in them.

In early Rome, highrises with several floors were constructed. In the lower floors of these buildings there were shops. They often had interior courtyards. Generally, these buildings were made of brick, with the upper floors made of wood.

These buildings were rented as apartments. In cities like Rome, populated by about a million inhabitants, people already knew about housing shortages. Rents could, therefore, be quite high.

Were there country houses?

The utilization of the country house (a secondary residence located far from the city and meant for relaxation) is typically Roman. Of course, in other civilizations, wealthy people had several residences or palaces. In Rome, from the end of the first century B.C., all rich Romans had one and often several houses in the country or at the seaside. Sometimes they even had small houses along the roads, where they could stop for a rest.

Did people pay taxes?

In the pharaohs' Egypt, money did not exist. Peasants paid their taxes with goods, giving up a share of their harvest and their herd.

Yes. Taxes represent a source of revenue for the government.

In some oriental societies, in Mesopotamia, and in Egypt, most land belonged to the rulers. Peasants who cultivated the land and the officials who administrated it were employees of the government. The officials took a share of the revenues and the land and gave the rest to the people who worked it. This system is similar to socialist countries of today. In ancient times, it brought wealth, from which most people benefited.

In Greece, the tax on wealth represented up to twenty percent of capital.

In Rome, tax on sales was very low, barely one percent. There was also a law concerning inheritances when they did not go directly from the parents to the children. This tax was five percent.

Taxes have steadily increased since ancient times.

Egyptian soldiers, armed with spears and shields.

Were there wars?

Two Greek infantrymen—armed with swords, spears, and shields—confront each other.

Yes. Unfortunately, wars have been fought since the dawn of mankind. Sometimes war results from a disagreement between two nations. Sometimes it is a desire for conquest. Other causes are the desire for more land, wealth, power, and security. In Persia, an aristocracy of nobles dominated. For centuries, these noblemen formed the mainstay of an army. The same was true for the knights of the Middle Ages, who went to battle on horses. They brought along people recruited from their entourage or peasants.

In Egypt and Mesopotamia, soldiers were taken from among the peasants. The officers were men who had been trained for war since childhood. They often knew how to read and write.

In Greece and Rome, all citizens did their military service and were expected to defend their homeland. In Sparta, they remained mobilized almost all their lives.

Career soldiers who were paid to fight were called *mercenaries*. From the time of the pharaohs' Egypt, there have been mercenaries in the armies.

Certain cultures—the Greeks, the Gauls, and the Iberians—were known for the quality of their soldiers. They supplied many mercenaries.

Glossary

A.D. *anno Domini,* in the year of the Lord. In a specified year of the Christian era.

amateur engaging in a science or project as a pastime rather than as a profession.

ancient a very early time in history beginning with the earliest known civilizations and extending to the fall of the Western Roman Empire in A.D. 476.

archaeological research finding ancient objects to collect or reproduce in a modern way; excavations or digs of ancient sites in a scientific manner.

archaeologist a person who undertakes the scientific study of material remains and the activities of a past life.

architect a person who designs buildings and advises in their construction.

Assyriologist an archaeologist who specializes in the study of Assyria.

atrium a rectangularly-shaped open patio around which a house is built.

B.C. *before Christ.* Occurring during the time before Christ was born.

carbon 14 a scientific method to determine the approximate age of material of biological origin such as bones or wood.

catastrophe a tragic event or disaster.

civilization an area with a high level of cultural and technological development.

Coptic the language of Egyptian Christians.

cuneiform writing writing composed of or written in wedge-shaped characters.

decipher to decode or convert to intelligible form.

dendrochronology the study of growth rings in trees or wood to determine the age of the specimen.

Egyptologist an archaeologist who specializes in the study of Egypt.

epigraphist a person who deciphers ancient inscriptions.

excavate to dig out and remove.

exhume to bring back from neglect or obscurity.

facade a false or artificial front, appearance, or effect.

grid a network of uniformly-spaced horizontal and perpendicular lines making it possible to identify a certain location.

grotto a cave or an artificial recess.

Hellenist an archaeologist who specializes in the study of Greece.

hieroglyphics written in a system of mainly pictorial characters.

hypothesis an assumption made in order to test its logical consequences.

Latinist an archaeologist who specializes in the study of Rome.

mausoleum a large tomb with places for entombment of the dead above ground.

mercenary an individual who serves merely for monetary compensation.

meticulous marked by extreme care in the consideration or treatment of objects or details.

microorganism a living organism of microscopic size.

mummy a body embalmed or treated for burial with preservatives.

necropolis a large, elaborate cemetery of an ancient city.

numismatist an expert in the study of coins, tokens, and paper money.

papyrus a plant that is cut into strips to make material on which to write.

pharaoh a ruler of ancient Egypt.

pillage the act of looting or plundering.

prehistorian a scientist who specializes in the study of living things and culture before history was written down.

preserve to treat in a certain way to protect the object from decomposition.

prospecting investigating and researching the area before an archaeological dig begins.

pyramid an ancient massive structure with a square bottom and four triangular sides.

raffia the fiber of the raffia palm used for making baskets and hats.

relic a remnant left over after its surroundings have decayed, disintegrated, or disappeared.

relief a type of sculpture in which forms or figures protrude from the flat plane.

Rosetta stone a stone found in 1799 that contains hieroglyphics and which provided the first clue to the deciphering of Egyptian hieroglyphics.

ruins the remains of something from the destroyed ancient world.

sieve a device with a mesh through which finer particles of a mixture are passed to separate them from coarser ones.

stratigraphical excavation archaeological digging by levels deep in the ground.

tell an ancient mound composed of remains of previous civilizations.

terra-cotta a glazed or unglazed fired clay used in the making of pottery or used for architectural purposes.

thermoluminescence a technique used to determine the dates of origin of pottery, tiles, and clay artifacts.

treasures precious objects, not only because they might be made of gold or silver, but also because the works are testimony to exceptional beauty and art.

volcano a vent in the crust of the earth from which lava and steam burst forth.

INDEX